# 20 Answers

&

# Apparitions & Revelations

## Michael O'Neill

Catholic
Answers
Press

*20 Answers: Apparitions & Revelations*
**Michael O'Neill**
© 2017 Catholic Answers

Published by Catholic Answers, Inc.
2020 Gillespie Way
El Cajon, California 92020
1-888-291-8000 orders
619-387-0042 fax
catholic.com

Printed in the United States of America

978-1-68357-036-3
978-1-68357-037-0 Kindle
978-1-68357-038-7 ePub

## Introduction

Miraculous messages from God can be attractive, inspirational, and transformative. They can bolster our faith and assure us that God loves us. For people who have left the Catholic faith, stories of divine intervention can be that nudge that brings them home. For those from other faith traditions, such stories can be a reason to take a closer look at the Church. Even skeptics and atheists want to have an explanation for the inexplicable.

Yet, for all the reasons to be excited, when it comes to reports of extraordinary communication from God—apparitions of God, Mary, or the saints, locutions, and other alleged supernatural phenomena—we have as many reasons to be cautious. When we're faced with apparent works of God, the Bible advises us to "test everything" (1 Thess. 5:21), for the world is also full of false prophets and confused souls.

Why does God sometimes communicate with us in these extraordinary ways? What does he want to tell us? How can we, along with the Church, discern the true from the false, and profit spiritually from what is true?

In this booklet we will look at the history and common characteristics of private revelation and miraculous apparitions, examine the ways that the Church evaluates these phenomena, and consider how they can deepen our faith and draw us closer to Christ. For, as St. Paul exhorts to the Thessalonians, we are not only to "test everything" but also to "hold fast what is good."

## 1. What is private revelation?

Of all the supernatural phenomena the Catholic Church has investigated throughout its history, the most complicated are those that deal with private revelations—messages that people, holy and otherwise, have attributed to God, the Virgin Mary, or the saints.

Private revelation is different from public revelation, which comes to us from God through Sacred Scripture and Sacred Tradition—valid for all time and meant for all, it ceased with the death of the last apostle. All revelatory miracles and messages that have occurred since are considered *private* revelation. Such messages do not belong to the deposit of faith, and belief in them—even those approved by the Church—is not required.

*The Catechism of the Catholic Church* (CCC) states:

Throughout the ages, there have been so-called "private" revelations, some of which have been recognized by the authority of the Church. They do not belong, however, to the deposit of faith. It is not their role to improve or complete Christ's definitive Revelation but to help live more fully by it in a certain period of history. Guided by the magisterium of the Church, the *sensus fidelium* knows how to discern and welcome in these revelations whatever constitutes an authentic call of Christ or his saints to the Church (67).

In his apostolic exhortation *Verbum Domini*, Pope Benedict XVI speaks of the unique value of private revelation:

The value of private revelations is essentially different from that of the one public revelation: the latter demands faith. . . . Private revelation is an aid to this faith, and it demonstrates its credibility precisely because it refers back to the one public revelation. . . . A private revelation can introduce new emphases, give rise to new forms of piety, or deepen older ones. It can have a certain prophetic character and can be a valuable aid for better understanding and living the gospel at a certain time; consequently, it should not be treated lightly. It is a help which is proffered, but its use is not obligatory.[1]

The dogmatic constitution *Dei Filius* from the First Vatican Council (1869–1870) reminds us that miracles are external signs God provides as arguments on behalf of revelation[2] and condemns any denial of the possibility of miracles, an error that would put a person outside communion with the Church:

If anyone should say that there can be no miracles,

and that all accounts of them, even those contained in Sacred Scripture, are to be thought of as fables and myths; or that miracles cannot be certainly known; or that they can never be rightly used to prove the divine origins of the Christian religion: let him be anathema.[3]

While it is necessary to establish the proper role of miraculous phenomena as leading the faithful to Christ, it would be a mistake to underestimate and devalue the importance of miracles in the life and history of the Church. They inspired the earliest Christians to follow Christ and have bolstered the faith of believers ever since.

## 2. Why would God work in this way?

God has always used signs and wonders to help plant, grow, and protect the seeds of faith in believers. The wonders worked by Christ encouraged people to follow him, and history's greatest miracle—the Resurrection—changed mere curiosity into true belief in a divine intervention. The apostles took up Christ's mandate to work miracles, and the revelation of the Holy Spirit at Pentecost sent them out into the world.

Christianity began to spread through the efforts of St. Paul, but a vision of Christ was necessary to set him on his path of evangelization. In the midst of persecution of the followers of Christ, the Roman emperor

Constantine was impelled to legalize Christianity in the year A.D. 312 after witnessing a miraculous symbol of Christ in the sky.[4]

Aside from the foundational role of miracles in the early centuries of Christianity, the results of revelations continue to impact Catholics even today. Many Catholics wear the Miraculous Medal, designed after the apparition of Mary to St. Catherine Labouré, or the brown scapular, believed to have been given to St. Simon Stock in visions by Our Lady of Mount Carmel.

When we pray the rosary, we implicitly recall that in 1208 St. Dominic received this devotion in a vision, and between the decades we pray the Fatima prayer,[5] given to the child visionaries in 1917. The popular Divine Mercy chaplet prayed at 3 p.m. by Catholics around the world derives from St. Faustina Kowalska's revelations from Jesus.

Believers have been strengthened in their faith by private revelations, and many conversions can be traced to their influence. In fact, conversions are among the spiritual fruits that are assessed in declaring phenomena worthy of belief. Nine million baptisms in Mexico City in the eight years following the messages of Our Lady of Guadalupe in 1531 speak to this important role.

The positive results of revelations can take a more concrete form: some of the most magnificent places of worship in the world are results of the Virgin Mary in her revelations requesting that they be built to honor her son. Four of the twelve largest church buildings in the world have such origins.

Throughout the Church's history, stories of revelations have been woven into the fabric of Catholic tradition and have played a significant role in the lives of the faithful. The insights and inspirations provided in miraculous events and messages have come at times of need for individuals, nations, and the universal Church.

## 3. What does Scripture teach us about private revelation?

Scripture gives us many passages that call us to reflect on the role of the supernatural in our lives of faith. St. Paul encourages us to be open to the supernatural when he reminds us, "Do not quench the Spirit, do not despise prophesying, but test everything, holding fast to what is good" (1 Thess. 5:19–21).

Although Christ worked many miracles of healing, he did not encourage the search for miracles: "An evil and unfaithful generation seeks a sign, but no sign will be given them except the sign of Jonah" (Matt. 16:4). Christ hints in a parable about Lazarus that even other-worldly revelations will not persuade the world: "If they will not listen to Moses and the prophets, neither will they be persuaded if someone should rise from the dead" (Luke 17:31). When the resurrected Christ addresses Thomas, he seems to be addressing us if we seek signs and wonders in our own day: "Have you come to believe because you have seen me? Blessed are those who have not seen and have believed" (John 20:29).

Despite asking us not to rest our faith entirely on miracles and not to get swept up in pursuing them, Jesus used miracles to draw people to him and encourage their faith. Even in our modern world, for many people miracles are a connection to the supernatural that might inspire or enliven their belief and participation.

From the beginning of Scripture, God reveals himself to humanity in major moments, from interactions with Adam in the creation account, to Noah at the time of the Great Flood, to Moses, upon whom he bestows the Ten Commandments. There are at least 120 instances of revelation (dreams and visions) mentioned in the Old Testament.[6]

Perhaps the Bible's most famous dreamer was Joseph, son of Jacob and Rachel, who shared his revelations with his family, which resulted in his brothers' plotting his death (Gen. 37:1–11). In one dream, the brothers of Joseph gathered bundles of grain that bowed to his own bundle. In another, the sun (his father), the moon (his mother), and eleven stars (his brothers) bowed down to Joseph himself.

Revelations continue in the New Testament. At the baptism of Christ, a voice from the heavens said, "This is my beloved Son, with whom I am well pleased" (Matt. 3:17). At the Transfiguration, in which Jesus is made to appear radiant atop a mountain, the prophets Moses and Elijah appear with Jesus (Matt. 17:1–9; Mark 9:2–8; Luke 9:28–36). A voice from the sky again calls him "Son."

The most famous apparitions in Scripture are the numerous times Christ appeared to the apostles (1 Cor. 15:5) and other times to various disciples, including on the road to Emmaus (Luke 24:13–35). In the early Church, the deacon Stephen saw a vision of the heavens open and Christ at the right hand of God the Father (Acts 7:55–56). The "visions and revelations" from the Lord (2 Cor. 12:1–6) are the impetus for the conversion of Saul (Gal. 1:11–16), setting him on the path to become Paul, the greatest missionary in Christian history. The final book of the New Testament, Revelation, relates the visions of St. John.

The revelations of the Bible received by prophets and apostles showcase a supernatural connection between the Church and the divine. Throughout Christian history, there have been stories of visions and divine messages, the most common being those attributed to the Virgin Mary. Some Protestants, skeptical of the power and significance that Catholicism affords her, may doubt these reports, but the scriptural basis for Mary's role in her son's saving work cannot be ignored:

- Through her, God the Father sent Christ to us physically.

- Elizabeth received the grace of God through the mouth of Mary (Luke 1:44).

- Jesus' first miracle—the wedding feast at Cana—and the beginning of his public ministry came at her request (John 2:4).

- From the cross, Jesus made her the mother of St. John, the beloved disciple, and thus the mother of all believers (John 19:26–27).

Although Jesus Christ is the sole mediator between God and man (1 Tim. 2:5–6), St. Paul has no problem asking the rest of us (including Mary) to be subordinate mediators as he asks us to pray for each other (Rom. 1:9; 1 Thess. 5:25; 1 Tim. 2:1). When we embrace the messages of Church-approved revelations of Jesus, Mary, and the saints, and reflect on the scriptural accounts of God's tangible intrusions in the human experience, we appreciate more deeply God's fatherly care for us and better understand his plan for salvation and our participation in it.

## 4. What are some examples of private revelation in history?

In addition to approving many apparitions of the Virgin Mary, the Catholic Church has recognized a few visions of Christ as authentic. Two of Catholicism's most famous and popular devotions, to the Sacred Heart of Jesus and the Divine Mercy, come from the visions of Jesus to saintly nuns.

St. Margaret Mary Alacoque (1647–1690) of Paray-le-Monial, in Burgundy, France, saw Jesus four times between 1673 and 1675. He showed her his heart to demonstrate the greatness of his love and asked her to spread the devotion. In his papal bull *Auctorem Fidei*, Pope Pius VI praised devotion to the Sacred Heart; and Leo XIII, in his encyclical *Annum Sacrum* (May 25, 1899), as well as on June 11 of that year, consecrated every person to the Sacred Heart.

The Divine Mercy devotion comes from apparitions of Jesus that St. Faustina Kowalska (1905–1938) experienced. The Polish nun reported several encounters with Jesus, which she recounted in her diary, later published as *Diary: Divine Mercy in My Soul*. The three main themes of the devotion are to ask for and obtain the mercy of God, to trust in Christ's abundant mercy, and to show mercy. Given a mandate by Christ to create an image of him, Faustina worked with an artist from Lithuania to depict our Lord with rays of light emanating from his heart in red and white, which symbolize the "blood and water" John describes in his Gospel (19:34). The mystical writings of Faustina were initially suppressed due to a bad translation, but John Paul II canonized the "apostle of divine mercy" on April 30, 2000, with the first Sunday after Easter established as Divine Mercy Sunday.

Private revelations that do not include a visual manifestation are considered *locutions*. In her official Vatican biography, St. (Mother) Teresa of Calcutta (1910–1997) revealed that the inspiration for her charitable work was a locution received on September 10, 1946, during a train ride from Calcutta to Darjeeling for her annual retreat. Telling her, "I cannot go alone," Christ revealed his pain at the neglect of the poor, how much he suffered for them, and how much he wanted their love. St. Teresa was to establish a religious community, the Missionaries of Charity, dedicated to the service of the poorest of the poor.[7]

Whereas most locutions in modern times claimed to have Jesus or the Virgin Mary as their source, Mother Eugenia Elisabetta Ravasio (1907–1990), an Italian nun and mystic known for social work on the Ivory Coast, said she received messages from God the Father. Bishop Alexander Caillot of Grenoble, who was mentioned in the messages, after ten years of examination recognized these messages as supernatural,[8] making them the only reported private revelation from God the Father that a bishop has approved. In 1988, Cardinal Petrus Canisius van Lierde, vicar general for the Vatican City State, granted Mother Eugenia's book, *The Father Speaks to His Children*, an imprimatur.[9]

Throughout the ages, locutions have also been claimed to emanate from icons or statues. In a controversial modern example in Akita, Japan, in 1973, Sr. Agnes Sasagawa experienced a series of phenomena, including being healed from deafness and manifesting stigmata. The local bishop investigated her convent's wooden statue of the Virgin Mary, which had begun bleeding and weeping, and gave it a positive judgment. Sr. Agnes reported receiving locutions from Mary through the statue.

Perhaps the most famous locutions ever claimed were those of St. Joan of Arc (1412–1431), who said the Archangel Michael, St. Margaret, and St. Catherine instructed her to support Charles VII and recover France from the English in the Hundred Years' War. The young woman played a key role in the successful siege of Orléans and other swift victories leading to the coronation of Charles VII at Reims. After her capture, imprisonment, and trial, Joan was declared guilty of heresy and burned at the stake at age nineteen. Twenty-five years after her execution, Pope Callixtus III affirmed her innocence, reversed the charges against her, and declared her a martyr.

## 5. Aren't stories of private revelations merely remnants of a more credulous, unscientific age?

For skeptics and modernists, stories of miracles are at best legendary tales used by the Church to inspire the faith of its members and at worst means to manipulate the uneducated masses into obsequious religious practice. And although some Catholics and others see the modern Church focusing less on the supernatural and more on a reason-based practice of their religion, miracles continue to be important in the modern Church.

One obvious example is in the canonization process, where two verified miracles are required for a person to be declared a saint. In these causes, almost all such miracles are medical healings with no natural explanation. These cures must be instantaneous, lasting, and complete, with no other possible incident or illness having triggered the change. Most stringent of all, there can be no medical treatment related to the healing. A quorum of doctors on a medical committee called the *Consulta Romana* must validate an inexplicable cure before it may be considered part of an act of intercession of a would-be saint. Science is also applied in examining phenomena such as allegedly weeping statues or claims of eucharistic miracles. In some rare cases of the latter, scientists have examined the host and found human blood or heart muscle integrated into it.

But what about modern claims of private revelation? Does the Church simply ignore claims that rely solely on the testimony of a witness and have no scientific proof?

The modern Church is still very interested in private revelation. For example, in 2016 the apparitions at San

Nicolas, Argentina (1983 through 1990), were declared by Bishop Hector Cardelli to be supernatural events worthy of belief. Local bishops approved two older Marian apparition cases, those of Benedicta Rencurel in Le Laus, France (1664), and Adele Brise in Champion, Wisconsin (1859), in 2008 and 2010, respectively. We have already noted one of the most popular devotions in the Catholic Church, the Divine Mercy, based upon the private revelation of a twentieth-century Polish nun. She was the first saint canonized in the twenty-first century.

Indeed, since the beginning of the twentieth century local bishops have established ten apparitions as supernatural events, while Church authorities have granted at least twenty others permission for faith expression.[10] Four apparitions—those at Fatima, at Beauring and Banneux in Belgium, and at Kibeho, Rwanda—have been recognized with additional Vatican support. In April 2014, in a display of approval, Pope Francis urged the Rwandan bishops to be agents of reconciliation, commending them to the Marian apparition at Kibeho.[11]

Although Pope Francis has discouraged over-credulity when it comes to reports of apparitions,[12] he showed his support for Church-approved private revelation when he dedicated his papacy to our Lady of Fatima as one of the first acts of his pontificate and attended the hundredth-anniversary celebrations in

Portugal. In this he followed in the footsteps of Popes St. John Paul II and Benedict XVI, who both displayed a love for the Virgin Mary under this title.

Along with Fatima, the worldwide Church celebrates other significant instances of private revelation, with official dates on the Roman Calendar for the events of Lourdes, Guadalupe, Mount Carmel, and Divine Mercy.

## 6. How should we approach claims of private revelation?

Private revelation, although potentially energizing for our faith, comes with a certain amount of peril. There are charlatans in the world who claim a connection to the divine for attention or to swindle unsuspecting believers of their time and money. There are also pious frauds who may in good faith believe that they are hearing authentic locutions.

It is human nature to want to seek what is new, exciting, and not known to everyone. Some modern believers crave secret knowledge from private revelation or in mystical phenomena that the Church hasn't vetted. This can result in fanaticism or an apocalyptic view of current world events.

St. John of the Cross, one of the greatest of mystics in the history of the Church, strongly discouraged the seeking of private revelation. This Doctor of the

Church taught that union with God could be attained through the three theological virtues of faith, hope, and love, not through visions or miraculous phenomena. Such things are not part of the core of the spiritual life. St. John goes so far as to suggest that if a vision comes, the recipient should at first not accept the occurrence and begin to assess the veracity of the vision only if it comes again. Faith holds on, he suggests, without seeing proof; those who want visions want to see, not to believe without seeing.[13]

St. Teresa of Avila, a recipient of many visions, acknowledges that mystical experiences can be a great blessing when they are genuine and are appropriately discerned but cautions against seeking them out:

> I will only warn you that, when you learn or hear that God is granting souls these graces, you must never beg or desire him to lead you by this road. Even if you think it is a very good one . . . there are certain reasons why such a course is not wise. . . . It is true that to have these favors must be a very great help toward attaining a high degree of perfection in the virtues; but one who has attained the virtues at the cost of his own work has earned much more merit.[14]

Although it is the competence of the local bishop to investigate supernatural claims when they have an impact on the local Church community, he may not have the resources or time for a full investigation. The Church may move slowly out of prudence or because it is unable or unwilling to investigate something that most likely is not an authentic supernatural event. Of the thousands of such claims throughout history, Church authorities have approved only a handful. Because of this common delay when the faithful lack any guidance about how to approach a specific allegedly supernatural occurrence, it is important to proceed with caution and discernment.

Benedict XIV, who studied miracles extensively before becoming pope, commented that even some of the revelations of some saints "whose sayings and writings in rapture and derived from rapture are filled with errors."[15] It is important to remember as well that the recipients and relaters of prophecy are human and to see things from their own perspective. In his classic book on discerning private revelations, *A Still, Small Voice*, Fr. Benedict Groeschel quotes a Latin proverb to explain how the personal understandings and cultural experiences of the "prophet" creep into the prophecies given him by God: "That which is received is received in the manner of the receiver."[16]

Christian faith cannot accept revelations that claim to surpass or correct the revelation of which Christ is the fulfillment, as is the case in certain non-Christian religions and also in certain recent sects based on such "revelations." In general, our faith requires avoiding two extremes: an overemphasis and credulity regarding the supernatural on the one hand and the denial of the possibility of divine intervention on the other.

## 7. How does the Church judge claims of private revelation?

Church officials are called to assess the phenomena and the people who report them, looking for evidence of authenticity. Typically, if the situation merits it, the bishop will assemble a commission comprising a team of experts from various disciplines to create a report to advise him on how to render judgment. These experts may come from many fields—most typically theology, psychology, psychiatry, and anthropology.

The most recent document from the Congregation for the Doctrine of the Faith (CDF) that lays out the guidelines for the judgment of claims of private revelation is the *Normae Congregationis*, or "Norms of the Congregation for Proceeding Judging Alleged Apparitions and Revelations," approved by Pope Paul VI in 1978 and written in Latin for the eyes of bishops alone. The purpose of the document, as indicated by William Cardinal Levada in his introduction to the now publicly available document, is to

> aid the pastors of the Catholic Church in their difficult task of discerning presumed apparitions, revelations,

messages or, more generally, extraordinary phenomena of presumed supernatural origin. . . . [May it also] be useful to theologians and experts in this field of the lived experience of the Church, whose delicacy requires an ever-more thorough consideration.[17]

In section II, *Normae Congregationis* instructs the local bishop to take four steps with respect to a claim of private revelation. These can be summarized as follows:

1. Promptly gather the details of the case and be attentive to its development.

2. If the faithful seek it, allow and disseminate the devotion, providing that no negative aspects of the case have been found.

3. In serious matters, take action as necessary.

4. In cases that may present cause for concern but not a clear answer, do not intervene but remain attentive to its development.

Although the diocesan bishop possesses the right to initiate an investigation, that country's national conference of bishops may intervene at his request or at the request of a qualified group of faithful not "motivated by suspect reasons." Since the Church has no providential protection in the area of private revelation, the bishop could be in error. The Vatican may intervene if the situation involves the Church at large or if discernment requires it, but ordinarily it does not. The CDF judges the way the local ordinary conducted his investigation and decides whether it is necessary to initiate a new examination.

A modern example of the progression in the levels of intervening authority is the alleged apparitions of Mary at Medjugorje in present-day Bosnia and Herzegovina, which began in 1981. The local ordinary investigated and discouraged it. In 1991 the Zadar Commission of Yugoslavian bishops judged it to be "not established as supernatural," and a Vatican commission reexamined it from 2010 to 2014. At the time of this booklet's publication, the results of the commission are unknown.

There are three categories of judgment of the supernatural character of an event:

1. Not worthy of belief

2. Worthy of belief

3. Nothing contrary to the Faith

The negative judgment is given by the Latin formulation *Constat de non supernaturalitate*, that is, "It is established that there is nothing supernatural." The negative criteria delineated in *Normae Congregationis* are:

1. Glaring errors in facts

2. Doctrinal errors attributed to God or Mary

3. Pursuit of financial gain

4. Gravely immoral acts committed by visionary

5. Psychological disorders or tendencies in the visionary

The positive judgment that the event is worthy of belief is expressed by the Latin formulation *constat de supernaturalitate*, that is, "it is established that there is something supernatural." The positive criteria delineated in *Normae Congregationis* are:

1. There must be moral certainty—or at least great probability—that something miraculous has occurred. The commission may interview the visionaries, call other witnesses, and visit the site of the events.

2. The subject(s) who claim(s) to have had the apparition must be mentally sound, honest, sincere, of upright conduct, obedient to ecclesiastical authorities, and able to return to the normal practices of the Faith (such as participation in communal worship, reception of the sacraments, etc.).

3. The revelations must be theologically acceptable, morally sound, and free of error.

4. The apparition must result in positive spiritual assets that endure (e.g., prayer, conversion, and increase of virtue).

The third category is the one of uncertainty constituting a "wait and see" stance. This judgment is given in the form of the Latin phrase *non constat de supernaturalitate*, that is, "it is *not* established that there is something supernatural." The vast majority of investigated apparitions receive this assessment when the committee cannot come to a definitive conclusion. An apparition with such a designation might or might not be of supernatural origin. Although there is no proof of the phenomenon originating from anything but natural causes, none of the negative criteria are fulfilled, and the supernatural cause is not ruled out.

For an apparition to be declared authentic, it is not enough for the messages to be free from doctrinal error. There have been many claimed apparitions in which the messages are not contrary to the Faith, but other factors are present, such as the pursuit of financial gain, lack of obedience to ecclesial authority, or psychological conditions that rule out the possibility of a supernatural cause.

The local bishop will assess the best pastoral path forward and sometimes will give encouragement to the cultus (devotion) that has arisen around the alleged phenomenon. This does not mean he approves its supernatural character. At this stage, the associated messages may be approved for publication or pilgrimages allowed. In some cases, the local ordinary might deem it appropriate to consider the events worthy of faith expression. The bishop could opt to allow public devotion even as the events are ongoing, all the while keeping a watchful eye on his flock to make sure that they don't engage in something that puts their faith or well-being in peril. Because of the inherent dangers in unapproved events, many *non constat* cases result in the devotion being limited rather than encouraged.

In a very few cases, a subsequent local bishop has reversed a negative judgment. More common is when a "wait and see" apparition is upgraded to a positive one when further investigation is undertaken.

Although it is possible that a subsequent bishop could change a "worthy of belief" status to "not worthy of belief," the odds are practically zero. Such a decision would confuse the faithful and weaken the perception of authority of the Church in such matters. When an apparition's authenticity is called into question after a positive judgment, the devotion may not be encouraged or emphasized as much.

## 8. What are some of the characteristics of authentic private revelations?

The *Normae Congregationis* (see answer 7) sets out the procedures to be followed by Church officials in investigating the authenticity of extraordinary claims. Bishops evaluate the legitimacy of private revelation according to those guidelines.

When Church officials investigate private revelation, lack of humility in the seer is a red flag. Bishops often consulted St. Philip Neri (1515–1595) on the authenticity of mystics. With an eye to obedience and humility, he had great success in ferreting out frauds. For instance, in 1560, some cardinals were discerning about a nun who was having visions. They sought Philip's opinion, and he went to see the young sister. He said to her, "Sister, I didn't want to see you; I wanted to see the saint." The nun answered, "But I am the saint!" Philip reported confidently to the cardinals that her visions were not from God.[18]

In many of the cases that Church authorities reject, disobedience has been prevalent: for example, the alleged seer continuing to hold prayer meetings or other activities despite the instruction of the local bishop to stop.

Conversely, authentic mystics have shown obedience at times of great difficulty. Pope Benedict lauded the posture of St. Hildegard von Bingen, who became a Doctor of the Church:

As always happens in the life of true mystics, Hildegard too wanted to put herself under the authority of wise people to discern the origin of her visions, fearing that they were the product of illusions and did not come from God. . . . This is the seal of an authentic experience of the Holy Spirit, the source of every charism: the person endowed with supernatural gifts never boasts of them, never flaunts them and, above all, shows complete obedience to the ecclesial authority.[19]

The widely practiced devotion to the Sacred Heart of Jesus stems from the revelations of Jesus to the French nun St. Margaret Mary Alacoque in a series of apparitions from 1673 to 1675. On one occasion, Jesus told St. Margaret Mary to do something, but her superior did not approve it. Jesus reminded her:

Not only do I desire that you should do what your superior commands but also that you should do nothing of all that I order without their consent. I love obedience, and without it no one can please me.[20]

And later our Lord told her:

Listen, my daughter, and do not lightly believe and trust every spirit, for Satan is angry and will try to deceive you. So do nothing without the approval of those who guide you. Being thus under the authority of obedience, his efforts against you will be in vain, for he has no power over the obedient.[21]

Obedience played an important role in perhaps the most famous instance of the Church changing its stance in the assessment of private revelation: the Divine Mercy revelation to St. Faustina. Initially, the local bishop and the CDF placed prohibitions on the messages of the apparitions. This condemnation was lifted in 1978 through the work of St. John Paul II. Celebrated on the Sunday after Easter, Divine Mercy features specific indulgences that are awarded under the usual conditions. All these great honors and devotion occurred only after many years of Sr. Faustina obediently ceasing public celebration or distribution of the message found in her *Diary*. She wrote about the challenges of pride: "Satan can even clothe himself in a cloak of humility, but he does not know how to wear the cloak of obedience."[22]

St. Padre Pio, the famous Capuchin monk from Pietrelcina, Italy, is another exemplary model of obedience. Because of the public curiosity regarding his tremendous mystical gifts—reportedly including the stigmata, bilocation, and the ability to read souls—Church authorities suppressed his ability to say Mass publicly while they investigated him. He was obedient until his death in 1968 and was canonized in 2002.

Obedience aside, even private revelations received by canonized or otherwise highly regarded mystics can be flawed. Because imperfect humans receive the visions, what they do with those visions can be flawed. There are several potential causes of such error. For example, it can be due to a faulty interpretation of visions by the recipient. This is why reflections on the life and death of Christ, or other historic scenes, should be taken as approximations only, not word-for-word truth. St. Frances of Rome and Bl. Anne Catherine Emmerich have contradictions about the life of Christ in their visions. St. Catherine Labouré foretold many events correctly but failed on others.

A true revelation may be altered involuntarily by the recipient, especially in cases of interior locutions that needed to be translated into words. The famous mystic St. Bridget admits such a difficulty in recording her own revelations.[23] Similarly, those who record the revelations from the testimony of the visionary some-times modify them.

## 9. Do we have to believe in approved private revelations?

In a nutshell, no. But the Catholic Church has a simple and clear approach to how we should regard private revelation that has been investigated and ruled upon by the proper authorities.

If the competent ecclesial authority (typically the lo-cal bishop) has established a private revelation as wor-thy of belief, we may safely engage in it and incorporate it into our lives of faith. A positive judgment means that the associated message is not contrary to faith and morals. But because belief in a private revelation is not part of the deposit of faith, Catholics are at liberty to decide how much personal spiritual emphasis to place on apparitions and the messages they deliver. If we find it to be strange or unnecessary, we may disregard it.

However, without full knowledge of all the facts surrounding alleged phenomena, it is sensible for us to rely on the judgments of the ecclesial authority in providing pastoral guidance on these matters. As the bishops are entrusted with the responsibilities of discerning and ruling on apparitions, so too do members of the diocese have fundamental responsibilities.

According to the 1983 *Code of Canon Law*, the faithful are to obey their bishops when the latter act as Christ's representatives (canon 212)—that is, when they teach formally or establish binding discipline as pastors of their flock. This obedience is intended to promote the common good. Canon 753 also speaks of the "religious assent" owed to the bishops' teaching authority, which means a special quality of respect and gratitude, along with critical awareness and goodwill.

The bishop safeguards his flock from being exposed to theologically unsound private revelation or other dangers related to the pursuit of alleged phenomena. Canon law requires Catholics to be obedient to the discernment of the local bishop, which means that they should not publicly oppose a positive decision nor engage in a devotion that has received a negative judgment.[24]

The Catholic Church is so careful in judging alleged miracles that, at the *Consulta Romana* in the Vatican, only a small fraction of proposed medical miracles claimed to be worked through the intercession of a would-be saint get recognized as being without natural explanation. Likewise, at the famed apparition site of Lourdes many thousands of miracles have been claimed, but the Church has validated only sixty-nine cases.

## 10. What are Marian apparitions?

Throughout Christian history, there have been reports of supernatural, corporeal appearances of Jesus, the saints, and angels, but apparitions of the Virgin Mary are by far the most common. Typically they are accompanied by messages for the faithful, at times just for the witnesses themselves but in most other cases for a larger audience—the local community, the country, or the universal Church. We must answer the question of what should be the response to the instructions, prophecy, and warnings that are often found in the content of the messages.

In a 1973 pastoral letter on the Blessed Virgin Mary, the U.S. bishops commented on the value of understanding apparitions:

Authenticated appearances of Mary are "providential happenings [that] serve as reminders of basic Christian themes: such as prayer, penance, and the necessity of the sacraments."[25]

The Virgin often comes with a request—for instance, that a church be built to honor her son, as was the case in the Guadalupan events in Mexico City in the sixteenth century. In other cases she has come to bestow gifts on her children, such as the Miraculous Medal, the scapulars of different colors, and the Holy Face Medal. She has come with secrets and prophecies, as in the cases of Fatima in Portugal, La Salette in France, and Kibeho in Rwanda.

Although the clear purpose of Marian apparitions in general is to give people hope and draw them closer to Christ, it is important to keep a proper perspective, avoiding sensationalism and apocalyptic anxieties. Cardinal Ratzinger, the future Pope Benedict XVI, reminded the faithful of the proper perspective regarding apparitions:

> To all curious people, I would say I am certain that the Virgin does not engage in sensationalism; she does not act in order to instigate fear. She does not present apocalyptic visions but guides people to her son. And this is what is essential. The Madonna did not appear to children, to the small, to the simple, to those unknown in the world in order to create a sensation. Mary's purpose is, through these simple ones, to call the world back to simplicity, that is, to the essentials: conversion, prayer, and the sacraments.[26]

The Blessed Mother has intervened in human history on numerous occasions during times of greatest distress, such as war, famine, or plague. She has attended to the needs of people around the world in a way that only a mother could, adapting to the needs of her various children by showing in herself the physical traits, dress, and language that would be received best by those hearing her messages.

Sometimes the titles for Marian apparitions come from the places in which they occur; Our Lady of Knock (Ireland) and Our Lady of Lourdes (France) are famous examples. For others, the sobriquets are derived from the messages or other attributions to the apparition, such as Our Lady of Peace, Our Lady of the Miraculous Medal, or Our Lady with the Golden Heart. Sometimes two titles refer to the same event: Our Lady of the Rosary is the name given to Our Lady of Fatima.

Although most visionaries have been European females sixteen years of age or younger (at the time of the first apparition) and living as shepherds, students, or members of a religious community, visionaries have come in many varieties. St. Juan Diego was a fifty-seven-year-old man at the time of the apparitions of Our Lady of Guadalupe. Several popes have claimed visions of Mary; so did Bruno Cornacchiola, a man on his way to assassinate the pope in 1947 in Trefontane, Italy.[27]

Apparitions have played a role in the lives of many great saints. Several hundred saints have claimed to witness apparitions of our Lord, the Virgin Mary, or other saints. Eminent Mariologist Fr. René Laurentin's comprehensive work *Dictionary of Apparitions of the Virgin Mary* lists 308 saints with such an honor. Vocations have resulted from Marian apparitions (approximately one in every seven of the approved visionaries), such as Alphonse Ratisbonne becoming a priest after his experience in Rome in 1842, or St. Bernadette Soubirous of Lourdes and Lucia dos Santos of Fatima becoming nuns.

The experiences of visionaries are vastly different, especially regarding the duration of the apparitions and the time span over which they occur. In some instances—such as the group apparitions at Knock and La Salette, and the single-visionary apparitions at Pont-main, France—the visionaries encountered the Virgin just once. In contrast, French shepherdess Benedicta Rencurel received thousands of apparitions of the Virgin from 1664 until the shepherdess died in 1718. The Blessed Mother asked that a church and a house for priests be built, with the intention of drawing people to greater conversion, especially through the sacrament of penance.

## 11. How many times has Mary appeared?

According to the *Dictionary of Apparitions of the Virgin Mary*, there have been approximately 2,500 reported Marian apparitions.[28] Miraclehunter.com identifies at least twenty-eight apparitions that were judged positively by a local bishop's commission, seventeen of which have received some form of Vatican recognition.[29] Fr. Laurentin reports that the Church recognizes fifteen apparitions, but Fr. Salvatore Perella, another Marian expert, says there are nine.[30] Because there is no formal process established in canon law for recognition of apparitions by the Vatican, interpretation of the signs of recognition by different scholars results in a variation in these numbers.

There are two distinct periods in the history of apparition approval connected to the manner in which they were investigated. Prior to the Council of Trent (1545–1563), which tasked local bishops with investigating local apparitions, visions were not examined through a formal process of inquiry. When approved, a vision would be celebrated on the local level with the construction of a shrine and the celebration of a regional feast or commemoration. In the sixteenth century and beyond, the investigative commissions of bishops have ruled on the veracity of alleged apparition events.

Since then, the number of reported visions has been fairly consistent. In the twentieth century, however, most notably since the 1980s, there has been a veritable explosion of alleged apparition activity. It is worth noting that very few modern apparitions enjoy approval. Subsequent to the investigation and approval of the local ordinary, the Vatican has given some form of recognition to four apparitions: Our Lady of Fatima (Portugal, 1917), the Virgin with the Golden Heart (Beauraing, Belgium, 1932), the Virgin of the Poor (Banneux, Belgium, 1933), and Mother of the Word (Kibeho, Rwanda, 1981).

Six additional apparitions have been investigated and approved by the local ordinary without having yet received formal Vatican recognition: Our Lady of All Nations (Amsterdam, Holland, 1945), Our Lady of Akita (Akita, Japan, 1973), Our Lady Reconciler of Peoples and Nations (Betania, Venezuela, 1976), Our Lady of Cuapa (Cuapa, Nicaragua, 1980), Our Lady of the Rosary (San Nicolas, Argentina, 1983), and Our Lady, Queen of the Rosary (Itapiranga, Brazil, 1994).

Another twenty or so apparitions enjoy initial permission for faith expression from the local bishop, but their supernatural nature has not been verified. All in all, only about 4 percent of all reported apparitions in the twentieth century have received even the lowest level of approval of faith expression by the local ordinary.

The United States has experienced many alleged apparitions, starting with a legend involving its first president, George Washington.[31] But ecclesiastical authorities have approved only the 1859 apparitions to Adele Brise in Robinsonville, Wisconsin, as worthy of belief. Of the more than 100 claims of apparitions in the twentieth century, only the Our Lady of America apparitions in Ohio in the 1950s have received even an approval of faith expression.

With the proliferation of apparition reports at the end of the twentieth century, the Church reacted with concern about the effects of the focus on such phenomena. The U.S. bishops addressed this issue in a 1996 special assembly:

> Within the church community, the multiplication of supposed "apparitions" or "visions" is sowing confusion and reveals a certain lack of a solid basis to the faith and Christian life among her members. On the other hand, these negative aspects in their own way reveal a certain thirst for spiritual things, which, if properly channeled, can be the point of departure for a conversion to faith in Christ.[32]

## 12. What are the common themes and messages of Marian apparitions?

Throughout Christian history, the messages of apparitions of the Virgin Mary have included a number of consistent themes. The excerpts below are from MiracleHunter.com, a website that catalogues these apparitions along with their histories and associated messages.

### Penance

In the apparitions to Benedicta Rencurel in 1664, the Blessed Mother asked for a church and a house for priests to be built, with the intention of drawing people to greater conversion, especially through the sacrament of penance. Numerous physical healings have been associated with the site, especially when oil from a lamp is applied to wounds according to the directives the Virgin Mary gave to Benedicta. She had visions throughout the second half of her life, making them the longest-running apparitions with Church approval, which came from the local bishop in 2008.

From November 29, 1932, to January 3, 1933, Mary appeared thirty-three times to five children at the playground of a convent school in Beauraing, Belgium. Identifying herself as "the Immaculate Virgin" and "Mother of God, Queen of Heaven," she called for prayer for the conversion of sinners.

### Gifts

Catherine Labouré, a novice in the order of the Sisters of Charity, received visions of St. Vincent and of Jesus present in the Eucharist before experiencing two apparitions of the Blessed Virgin Mary, including one detailing the design for a medal, later known as the Miraculous Medal, which has been reproduced over a billion times throughout the world.

### Conversion

Many Marian apparitions call for a conversion of heart. One great example was the apparition to Marie-Alphonse Ratisbonne, an anti-Catholic Jew who befriended a baron in Rome and began wearing the Miraculous Medal as a simple test. On January 20, 1842, while waiting for the baron in a church, Ratisbonne encountered a vision of the Blessed Virgin Mary. He converted to Catholicism, joined the priesthood, and began a ministry for the conversion of Jews.

*Peace*
During the devastation of the Franco-Prussian War, Mary appeared on a farm to students of a nearby convent school in France. Mary's message was written on a banner that unfurled from her feet: "But pray my children. God will hear you in a short time. My son allows himself to be moved by compassion." At 5:30 p.m. on the day of the apparition, the Prussian army halted its advance through France when the Prussian commander claimed to have seen an image of the Lady in the sky and refused to advance any further. A peace treaty between France and Prussia was signed eleven days later. All the soldiers from Pontmain returned unharmed.

*Silence*
In one of the most incredible reported Marian apparitions in history, our Lady is said to have appeared in Zeitun, Egypt, hovering above St. Mark's Coptic Church on many occasions over a span of three years beginning in 1968. She appeared especially at night, and sometimes white doves accompanied her. The apparitions attracted crowds as large as a quarter of a million people, including Christians, Jews, and

Muslims. The apparitions were photographed, filmed, and broadcast on Egyptian TV. An estimated forty million people witnessed the events.

In Knock, Ireland, in 1879, during a pouring rain, the figures of Mary, Joseph, John the Evangelist, and a lamb on a plain altar appeared over the gable of the village chapel, enveloped in a bright light. None of them spoke. Fifteen people, between the ages of five and seventy-five, saw the apparition.

*Prayer*

In all apparitions—most famously, Our Lady of Fatima requesting that the rosary be prayed for the conversion of sinners—the Virgin Mary asks for prayer. In one example from Gietrzwald, Poland, in 1877, approved by Pope St. John Paul II when he was a cardinal, our Lady appeared to thirteen-year-old Justyna Szafrynska when she was returning home with her mother after having taken an exam prior to receiving her First Holy Communion.

The next day, while reciting the rosary, twelve-year-old Barbara Samulowska also saw the "bright Lady" sitting on a throne with the Infant Christ among angels over the maple tree in front of the church. The girls asked, "Who are you?" She answered, "I am the Blessed Virgin Mary of the Immaculate Conception." "What do you require, Mother of God?" they asked. Her answer: "I wish you to recite the rosary every day."

*Warnings*

The African apparitions in Kibeho, Rwanda, began in November 1981 when six young women and one boy claimed to see the Blessed Virgin Mary and Jesus. But only the visions of Mary to three—seventeen-year-old Alphonsine, twenty-year-old Nathalie, and twenty-one-year-old Marie Claire—have received their bishop's solemn approval. The Virgin appeared to them with the name *Nyina wa Jambo*, that is, "Mother of the Word," which, she explained, is synonymous with *Umubyeyl W'iamna*, "Mother of God." She asked the people to convert and change their ways and predicted a great tragedy with "rivers of blood." The Rwandan genocide followed shortly thereafter, proving this to be an authentic appearance of Mary and causing Bishop Augustin Misago of Gikongoro, Rwanda, to declare: "Yes, the Virgin Mary did appear in Kibeho on Nov. 28, 1981" over "the course of the following six months."

*Healing*

The Church often views healings as good fruits associated with an apparition event that go toward a formal approval. Most apparition sites have a reputation for healings, but the most famous example, of course, is that of Our Lady of Lourdes in France. At the Grotto of Massabielle, the Virgin showed herself eighteen times to young teenager Bernadette Soubirous. Under the title "the Immaculate Conception," she called for penance and prayer for the conversion of sinners. The International Medical Association at Lourdes has noted more than 7,000 remarkable cures.

In Filippsdorf in the Czech Republic in the year 1866, Magdalene Kade, a woman bedridden due to many illnesses, received a vision of the Blessed Virgin, who immediately cured her. A bishop's commission examined the event and recognized the healing and the supernatural character of the apparition.

In another approved apparition, in Banneux, Belgium, in a garden behind the Beco family's cottage, the Blessed Mother is said to have appeared eight times to eleven-year-old Mariette Beco. Calling herself the "Virgin of the Poor," Mary promised to intercede for the poor, the sick, and the suffering.

*Sorrow*

The Virgin Mary has made known on many occasions her Sorrowful Heart in order that we might seek conversion. Perhaps the most famous examples are the apparitions of Our Lady of La Salette, high in the French Alps, where the Blessed Virgin Mary came to eleven-year-old Maximin Giraud and fourteen-year-old Melanie Calvat-Mathieu while they tended sheep. Sorrowful and tearful, she called for conversion and penance for sins. The local bishop said that it "has within itself all the characteristics of the truth, and the faithful are justified in believing it beyond doubt and for certain."

In 1608, a number of children were playing while tending their sheep in a field on the outskirts of the village of Siluva in Lithuania. They beheld a beautiful young woman standing on the rock holding a baby in her arms and weeping bitterly. The town, which had lost its Catholic identity to the Calvinists over the course of eighty years, was restored to the Faith.

*Request to Build a Church*
In the events on Mount Tepeyac in Mexico, the Virgin Mary proclaimed herself "the mother of the true God who gives life" and left her image permanently upon the *tilma* (cloak) of St. Juan Diego, a middle-aged man newly converted to Christianity. Her likeness was given as a sign to Bishop Zumárraga to construct a church on the site of the apparitions so that "her son be made manifest," an event that led to the conversion of millions of indigenous Aztecs in the decade following the event.

The request that a church be built is perhaps the most common message found in the apparitions of the Virgin Mary, with many of the shrines of Europe—such as Le Laus in France and Lejask in Poland—owing their existence to a request or miraculous sign from the Virgin.

## 13. What is the Miraculous Medal?

St. Catherine Labouré, a novice in the order of the Sisters of Charity, became known to the world for her prophetic visions of the Virgin Mary and for mystically receiving the design of a medal that would become the most famous of Catholic medals. Late one night, near the beginning of her novitiate, on July 18, 1830, she awoke and was led by a "shining child" to the convent chapel. There the Blessed Mother appeared, according to St. Catherine:

> The Virgin was standing. She was of medium height and clothed in all white. Her dress was of the whiteness of dawn, made in the style called *à la Vierge*, that is, high neck and plain sleeves. A white veil covered her head and fell on either side of her feet. Under the veil her hair, in coils, was bound with a fillet ornamented with lace, about three centimeters in height or of two fingers' breadth, without pleats, and resting lightly on the hair. Her face was sufficiently exposed, indeed exposed very well, and so beautiful that it seems to me impossible to express her ravishing beauty.[33]

Mary spoke for hours, telling Catherine that she would have to undertake a difficult task and prophesying the impending travails of France and of an unspecified future mission.

On November 27, Mary appeared in the same chapel in the form of a picture, standing on a globe, with shafts of light streaming from her hands, surrounded by the words *Ô Marie, conçue sans péché, priez pour nous qui avons recours à vous* ("O Mary, conceived without sin, pray for us who have recourse to thee"). On the reverse side was a capital M with a cross above it and two hearts, one thorn-crowned and one pierced with a sword. Catherine heard a voice give these instructions:

> Have a medal struck after this model. All who wear it will receive great graces; they should wear it around the neck. Graces will abound for persons who wear it with confidence. This globe which you see is the world, France in particular, and for every person living in it. I am praying for it and for everyone in the world. The rays which shed on the globe from my hands are the graces which I bestow for all those who ask for them. But there are no rays that come from some of the gems (from my fingers) because those are the graces which God wishes to bestow on them but they forget to ask.[34]

Catherine confided the events to her confessor, Fr. Aladel, and he, convinced of her sincerity, persuaded Archbishop de Quélen of Paris to give permission for a medal to be struck. Within the first two years, 50,000 medals were given out. The popularity of the medal grew, especially after the conversion of Alphonse Ratisbonne in 1842.

In 1836, the archbishop initiated an official canonical inquiry into the alleged visions. Catherine refused to appear, wishing her identity to be kept a secret. Fr. Aladel pleaded to be allowed to keep her name anonymous. The tribunal, basing its opinion on the stability of her confessors and Catherine's character, decided to favor the authenticity of the visions:

> [T]he vision could not be purely imaginary, having appeared several times. . . . She was not the effect of a dream or the product of an excited imagination, which took place during the day, during prayer or Mass. . . . The effects of the medal . . . seem to be the means by which the sky seems to have confirmed the reality of the vision, the truth of the words of the visionary and have approved the draft and the spread of the medal.[35]

On July 13, 1836, Archbishop de Quélen approved the visions as authentic.

Catherine worked for another forty-six years in the hospices of her order, engaging in menial tasks such as taking care of patients and looking after chickens. Not until a few months before her death in 1876 did she reveal herself as a visionary to anyone (except her confessor, Fr. Aladel, and her superior, Sr. Dufé), and she encouraged construction of a "Virgin of the Globe" statue. Her body lies incorrupt at the site of the apparition. Her coffin was severely damaged by moisture, but the saint inside was discovered to be in perfect condition.[36]

Pope Pius XII canonized Catherine on July 27, 1947.

## 14. What happened at Guadalupe?

There were actually two apparitions of Our Lady of Guadalupe more than two centuries apart. In 1326 in Cácerces, Spain, according to legend, the Virgin Mary appeared to a cowherd named Gil Cordero as he searched for a lost cow. The Virgin led him to a mound of stones, where he saw his cow lying motionless, as if dead. Cordero was preparing to cut off its hide when it awoke. Mary told him to dig at the spot.

Skeptical at first, local authorities dug to remove the stones and found a cave that contained a statue with an ancient document explaining its origin: it was a famous wonder-working statue that Pope Gregory the Great had sent to Spain 800 years earlier. A church and later a basilica were built, helping to make the devotion to Our Lady of Guadalupe one of the most popular in all of Spain and a favorite Marian title of Christopher Columbus, who dedicated an island he discovered to her patronage.

This devotion predates the more famous Mexican one of the same name. The Virgin was also called "Our Lady of Guadalupe" in Mexico because—according to some explanations—the visionary St. Juan Diego called her *Coātlaxopeuh*, meaning in his native Nahuatl "the one who crushes the serpent," and to the Spanish ear that sounded like Guadalupe, an already familiar name.

In December 1531, the Blessed Mother appeared several times on Tepeyac Hill to Juan Diego (1474–1548), an indigenous Mexican convert to Christianity, requesting that a temple be built there in order to honor her son. She comforted Juan in his doubt:

> Am I not here, I, who am your mother? Are you not under my shadow and protection? Are you not in the hollow of my mantle, the crossing of my arms? Am I not the source of all your joy? What more do you need? Let nothing else worry you, disturb you.

His persistence in attempting to persuade the Spanish bishop-elect in Mexico to begin this great undertaking was received favorably only when, during an audience, the devout native unfurled his *tilma*, which contained Castilian roses blooming out of season in winter and was emblazoned with an image of the Mother of God in native garb.

The wondrous image on Juan Diego's cactus-fiber cloak, which should have decayed within decades, remains to this day. Numerous copies have been made over the years to try to match its beauty and simulate its preservation. One copy, created in 1789, was painted on a similar coarse-fiber surface and placed in glass next to the *tilma*. It lasted eight years before the heat and conditions caused it to be taken down due to the fading of its colors and fraying of its threads.

Adolfo Orozco, a researcher and physicist at the National University of Mexico, sees no explanation for how the *tilma* remained intact despite having been "exposed for approximately 116 years without any kind of protection, receiving all the infrared and ultraviolet radiation from the tens of thousands of candles near it and exposed to the humid and salty air around the temple."[37]

The *tilma* has survived more than the ravages of Mexico's heat and humidity and the smoke of votive candles. In 1785, a worker accidentally spilled nitric acid solution onto a large portion of the image while cleaning the frame. It should have been eaten away almost immediately, but the image remains in good condition. In 1921, an anti-Church activist placed dynamite in a rose display at the altar of the Basilica of Our Lady of Guadalupe. When the explosion went off, the marble of the altar and floor were destroyed and the nearby metal crucifix mangled, but the image itself stayed intact.

It has become the most famous Marian image and belongs to a rare group of miraculous images classified as *acheiropoieta* (Greek, "not made by human hands"). One of the great mysteries of the Guadalupan image is how it was created. The image on the *tilma* is composed of pigments that have not been identified by chemical analysis as the product of animal, vegetable, or mineral dye. No under-sketch has been identified below the painting.

On May 7, 1979, Philip Serna Callahan, an accomplished biologist and author of fourteen books and 200 scientific papers, was invited to conduct infrared photographic tests on the *tilma*.

> In terms of this infrared study, there is no way to explain either the kind of color pigments or the maintenance of color luminosity and brightness over the centuries.
>
> When consideration is given to the fact that there is no under drawing, sizing or over varnish, and the weave of the fabric itself is utilized to give the portrait depth, no explanation of the portrait is possible by infrared techniques. It is remarkable that after more than four centuries there is no fading or cracking of the original figure on any portion of the agave *tilma*, which should have deteriorated centuries ago.[38]

Some have suggested that the image contains embedded symbolic meanings for both the natives and Spaniards who have encountered it, acting as a catechetical device. Our Lady's pose, standing in front of the rays of the sun and on top of the moon and with the stars at her back on her mantle, suggests that she is greater than these celestial bodies, which were divine personages for the Aztec people. However, the eyes of the image are downcast and the head bowed, suggesting that the woman is not a god herself but standing humbly with hands in a prayerful posture before God. Even her feet are said by some to be in movement, portraying her as dancing in prayer.

Because of her dark skin and hair she is called *la morenita* ("the dark little one"), allowing the indigenous people to see her as one of their own. She is wearing a maternity belt to indicate that she is pregnant, and on her stomach is a glyph, the *Nahui Ollin*, a four-petaled flower indicating north, south, east, and west, or God in his omnipresence. Although every other glyph is repeated on her dress, this one is unique from any of the other arabesque designs in the image. As a result, she can be understood to be the Virgin Mother of God.

Study of the *tilma* by scientists and others has rendered some noteworthy discoveries. In 1981, Peruvian ophthalmologist Jose Aste Tonsmann published an analysis of high-resolution imaging that revealed in the pupils and corneas of the eyes of the Virgin on the *tilma* an image of thirteen people whose appearance is consistent with the moment of the story when the saint reveals the image to the bishop-elect and his attendants.

On December 22, 1981, at the Observatory Laplace in Mexico City, Fr. Mario Rojas and Juan Hernández Illescas, a medical doctor and amateur astronomer, analyzed the stellar arrangement that appears in the mantle of the Virgin. They concluded that the stars were consistent with what astronomers believe was in the sky above Mexico City on the day the apparition occurred: the winter-morning solstice of December 12, 1531, Saturday, at 10:26 a.m.

Our Lady of Guadalupe has become a symbol for the Mexican people, and millions of pilgrims, some traversing the plaza on their knees, visit her shrine annually. In his historic 1979 visit to the Basilica of Our Lady of Guadalupe in Mexico City, Pope St. John Paul II called her a "Star of Evangelization," knelt before her image, invoked her motherly assistance, and called upon her as Mother of the Americas.

## 15. What happened at Lourdes?

There may be no other place on Earth better known for miraculous medical healings than the Shrine of Our Lady of Lourdes in France. It was built to commemorate the 1858 apparitions of the Virgin Mary under the title "the Immaculate Conception" to Bernadette Soubirous, a fourteen-year-old girl from a destitute family in a small town in the French Pyrenees.

On February 11, 1858, she first encountered a woman in a golden cloud and prayed a rosary in her presence at the grotto. Her sister Marie told their mother about the incident, and her mother forbade Bernadette from returning to the grotto. A few days later, Bernadette and her sisters finally persuaded her mother to let her return, and she encountered the woman again. During a third vision, when the girl was accompanied by two influential ladies of the town, the woman asked her to come to the site another fifteen times and promised her happiness not in this world but in the next.

Large crowds of people accompanied Bernadette at future visions, including Pierre-Romaine Dozous, the town's most eminent doctor, who evaluated her and announced that there was no indication of "nervous excitement." In a subsequent test, he put her hand through the flame of a candle during her ecstasy, and she felt no pain and was not burned.

On February 25 the Virgin instructed Bernadette to dig in the mud, revealing an underground water source that became a place of healing. The woman identified herself on the Feast of the Annunciation as "the Immaculate Conception," and it was with this identification that the parish priest began to believe in the authenticity of the visions. During subsequent visions, Bernadette was asked to "kiss the ground on behalf of sinners," to tell the clergy that they should build a chapel at the grotto, and to instruct the people that they should come in procession to the chapel.

After the apparitions came to an end on July 16, Bernadette went to study at a hospice run by the Sisters of Nevers. Eight years later, she left Lourdes for the last time to join the sisters. She was given the name Sr. Mary Bernard and worked there as sacristan, avoiding publicity as best she could. She referred to herself as "a broom which our Lady used, but now I have been put back in my corner."

After an investigation into the apparitions, on January 18, 1862, the bishop of the Tarbes declared them authentic: "We judge that Mary Immaculate, Mother of God, really appeared to Bernadette Soubirous on February 11, 1858, and on subsequent days, eighteen times in all. The faithful are justified in believing this to be certain."[39] In 1876 the Basilica at Lourdes was consecrated, and the liturgical feast of Our Lady of Lourdes was established for February 11, approved by Pope Leo XIII and granted to the Diocese of Tarbes in the year 1890.

On April 16, 1879, Bernadette died at age thirty-five. She is buried in St. Gildard Convent in Nevers, where her body lies incorrupt. Pope Pius X canonized her on the feast of the Immaculate Conception in 1933.

Since the apparitions, millions of pilgrims to the site have followed the instruction of Our Lady of Lourdes to "drink at the spring and wash in it." There have been more than 7,000 medically inexplicable cures recorded.[40] The Lourdes Office of Medical Observations, where miracle claims can be submitted and verified, is located onsite. Only the smallest fraction has passed the rigorous tests and standards of approval. In 2013, the

Sanctuary of Lourdes announced the sixty-ninth official miracle: the curing of Danila Castelli, an Italian woman, on her visit to the shrine in 1989. Her cure from the spontaneous and severe blood pressure hypertensive crisis and other serious health problems were certified as "unexplained according to current scientific knowledge" and declared an authentic miracle by her bishop.[41]

## 16. What happened at Fatima?

In what is generally considered the greatest approved modern apparition of the Virgin Mary, three shepherd children reported that they saw the Mother of God on May 13, 1917, and on the thirteenth day of five subsequent months in the Cova da Iria area of Fatima, Portugal. While tending sheep in a field, ten-year-old Lucia dos Santos and her cousins, Francisco Marto, nine, and Jacinta Marto, seven, saw "Our Lady of the Rosary" dressed all in white, "more brilliant than the sun, shedding rays of light clearer and stronger than a crystal glass filled with the most sparkling water and pierced by the burning rays of the sun."[42]

In these visions, Mary asked the children to pray the rosary daily for the conversion of sinners. She asked for prayer, penance, and the consecration of Russia to her Immaculate Heart.

On October 13, the Virgin appeared to the children for the sixth time, this time with St. Joseph, calling herself "Our Lady of the Rosary." The well-documented Miracle of the Sun ensued, in which the sun danced and seemed to descend on the onlookers drying the ground that had been covered with rain puddles. A crowd of 70,000 people witnessed the miracle, and, after the clouds of a rainstorm parted, numerous witnesses—some as far as forty miles away—reported seeing the sun dance, spin, and send out colored rays of light.

Fatima is an important place of pilgrimage, with five million people annually coming to the Basilica of Our Lady of the Rosary, construction of which began in 1928 and which was consecrated in 1956 by Cardinal Cerejeira, the patriarch of Lisbon.

As foretold by the Virgin, the two younger children did not live long. Bedridden, Francisco requested his First Communion, and the following day—April 14, 1919—he died. Jacinta died the following year after suffering a long illness.

At age eighteen, Lucia became a postulant at the convent of the Dorothean Sisters at Pontevedra, Spain, where the messages continued. The Virgin Mary gave her the devotion of the Five First Saturdays of each month by going to confession and receiving Holy Communion to make reparation to the hearts of Jesus and Mary.

Dom Jose Alves Correia da Silva, bishop of the Diocese of Leiria-Fatima, announced the results of the Investigative Commission on October 13, 1930, declaring the apparitions "worthy of belief." Every pope since has recognized the miraculous nature of the events and has emphasized the importance of the messages of Fatima.

Mary gave the children a secret in three parts. The first part of the secret—a vision of hell—revealed the tragic consequences of failure to repent and what awaits them in the invisible world if they are not converted. In the second part, she said: "You have seen hell where the souls of poor sinners go. To save them, God wishes to establish in the world devotion to my Immaculate Heart." Mary spoke of a war that "will break out during the pontificate of Pius XI." This was, of course, World War II, which Sr. Lucia reckoned as having been occasioned by the annexation of Austria by Germany during the reign of Pius XI.[43]

Our Lady also said that this would happen after a night of the "unknown light." Sr. Lucia pointed to January 25, 1938, when Europe was witness to a spectacular nighttime display of light in the sky. She wrote in her third memoir:

Your excellency is not unaware that, a few years ago, God manifested that sign, which astronomers chose to call an aurora borealis. . . . God made use of this to make me understand that his justice was about to strike the guilty nations. Our Lady added: "If my requests are heeded, Russia will be converted, and there will be peace; if not, she will spread her errors throughout the world, causing wars and persecutions of the Church. The good will be martyred; the holy father will have much to suffer; various nations will be annihilated. In the end, my Immaculate Heart will triumph. The holy father will consecrate Russia to me, and she shall be converted, and a period of peace will be granted to the world."[44]

On May 13, 2000, with Sr. Lucia in attendance, Pope St. John Paul II revealed the third part of the secret as containing the image of a "bishop in white" being shot. Since Mehmet Ali Ağca had wounded John Paul II in an assassination attempt in St. Peter's Square on May 13, 1981 (the feast of Our Lady of Fatima), the pope believed the secret applied to himself. He had the bullet that had pierced his body placed in the crown of the famed statue Our Lady of Fatima in Portugal. Sr. Lucia agreed with the pope's interpretation of events.

In *Crossing the Threshold of Hope*, the pope expressed his belief in Fatima this way: "And what are we to say of the three children from Fatima? . . . They could not have invented these predictions. They did not know enough about history or geography, much less about social movements and ideological developments. And nevertheless it happened just as they said."[45]

He also beatified the two deceased seers, Jacinta and Francisco, and made the feast day of Our Lady of Fatima universal by ordering it to be included in the

Roman Missal. In 2008, Pope Benedict XVI lifted the normal five-year waiting period to begin the canonization process of Sr. Lucia dos Santos, who died at ninety seven in 2005. On May 13, 2017, the centenary of the first Fatima vision of the Virgin Mary, Pope Francis canonized the Marto siblings.

## 17. What happened at Zeitun?

In most apparitions, our Lady appears to a few visionaries and leaves a series of messages with them. In Zeitun, Egypt, in the 1960s, something very different happened: The Virgin Mary reportedly appeared silently hovering above St. Mark's Coptic Church, visible to many people for a span of three years.

In the first apparition, on April 2, 1968, Mary reportedly appeared on the roof in a kneeling position, surrounded by light. She was wearing a long robe extending to below her feet. At times bright stars surrounded her, and at other times she had a shawl about her head and her hands were extended forward. The Virgin would walk over the church, especially over the middle dome, to bow in front of the cross that also shone with a bright light. She sometimes appeared with a child in her arms.

The first man who saw her, a Muslim named Farouk Mohammed Atwa, was undergoing operations for gangrene. The following day, when he went to hospital for his scheduled operation, he was certified completely healed.

The Virgin Mary was said to have appeared on many occasions through 1971, especially at night, sometimes accompanied by white doves that would fly around her. These appearances took place two or three times a week and attracted large crowds, sometimes as many as 250 thousand people. Christians, Jews, Muslims, and unbelievers gathered to view the sight. City officials cut the power in order to expose what they expected to be a hoax, but the supernatural lights continued. The apparitions were photographed, filmed, and broadcast on Egyptian TV. An estimated forty million people witnessed the events.[46]

Anba Kyrillos VI, the Coptic pope of Alexandria, delegated a commission of priests to research and investigate the phenomenon. They stayed for several nights until they saw with their own eyes the Blessed Virgin's apparition in full form moving on the domes and blessing the multitudes in front of the church. On May 5, 1968, Kyrillos VI said in an official statement, "The Blessed Virgin Mary has appeared several times on the Coptic Orthodox Church named after her at Zeitun in Cairo."[47]

The apparitions were also confirmed by the Jesuit priest Henry Ayrout and by nuns from the Society of the Sacred Heart, who witnessed the phenomenon and sent a detailed report to the Vatican, resulting in the arrival of an envoy, Cardinal Stephanos, on April 28, 1968. The cardinal also saw the apparitions and sent a report to Pope Paul VI in May.

The Zeitun events were not the only time that the Coptic Orthodox Church, through its validation process, which relies only on prayerful discernment, has recognized visible Marian apparitions as authentic. Others are said to have occurred at Edfu (1982), Shoubra (1986), Shentena Al-Hagger (1997), Assiut (2000), and Warraq el-Hadar (2009).[48]

## 18. Are private revelations happening in the world today?

Since the year 2000, at least forty Marian apparitions have been claimed. Given their recent occurrence, it is to be expected that the Church has not judged any of them as authentic. A few high-profile cases—such as those of Maria Divine Mercy; Borg-in-Nadur, Malta; and Charlie Johnston of Denver, Colorado—the Church has judged (in 2014, 2016, and 2017, respectively) as being not of supernatural origin. The other cases do not merit investigation or are being looked at by Church authorities without an official judgment having been given. The locutions claimed by Anne, a Lay Apostle (Kathryn Ann Clarke), while not established as supernatural, received an imprimatur on the content of messages from Leo O'Reilly, bishop of the Diocese of Kilmore, Ireland, in 2011.

Three cases since 2009 received positive judgments establishing them as supernatural events. On May 31, 2009, Archbishop Carillo Gritti of Itacoatiara, Brazil, approved the visions of Mary as Queen of the Rosary to twenty-two-year-old Edson Glauber.[49] Surprisingly, the visions were approved while they continued, but only for the years 1994 through 1998. After many years of pastoral verification, the archbishop stated: "Everything leads me to find that there is in the appearances of Itapiranga a supernatural origin." A future statement will be required to assess the apparitions that followed those bracketed years. The Virgin Mary was said to have appeared as a beautiful seventeen-year-old girl, occasionally with the Child Jesus in the arms of St. Joseph, and to have spoken of the consecration to his most chaste heart.

Another rare case of apparitions being approved while they continue is that of Gladys Quiroga de Motta, a housewife and grandmother from San Nicolas, Argentina. She has no formal education and no knowledge of the Bible or theology but claims to have received daily messages since 1983. The messages contain a call to conversion and prayer but also warn of future events and difficulties for the world. Gladys reportedly also received seventy-eight messages from Jesus Christ. Numerous healings, including the cure of a boy with a brain tumor, have been documented. More than 1,800 messages given daily over seven years were recognized as authentic.

On May 22, 2016, the bishop of San Nicolas, Héctor Sabatino Cardelli, released a statement of approval, declaring the visions to be "supernatural in character" and "worthy of belief." Further messages were reported in subsequent years, and the local ecclesial authorities are reviewing them.

More than a half-century old, the case of alleged visions of the Virgin Mary appearing in 1948 to Carmelite novice Teresita Castillo (1927–2017) in Lipa, Philippines, was reopened and reexamined by then-archbishop of Lipa, Ramon C. Arguelles. He undertook this investigation despite the Vatican's 2010 affirmation[50] of a 1951 negative ruling[51] on the apparition stating "there was no supernatural intervention in the reported extraordinary happenings including the shower of rose petals in Lipa."

On September 12, 2015, as part of the feast day celebrations in Lipa, Archbishop Arguelles released an official statement of approval, declaring "that the events and apparition of 1948 also known as the Marian phenomenon in Lipa and its aftermath even in recent times do exhibit supernatural character and is worthy of belief."[52] Three months later, however, in an unprecedented turn of events, the Congregation for the Doctrine of the Faith issued a statement[53] nullifying the bishop's approval.

In yet another report of a continuing mystical phenomenon coming from South America, since

1994 alleged stigmatic Catalina Rivas has claimed divine locutions. Archbishop René Fernández of Cochabamba gave them an imprimatur on April 2, 1998, and he approved the miraculous nature of an associated bleeding statue. But no declaration of supernaturality has been made on Rivas's stigmata or the locutions that she reports.

These are but a few of the many claims from around the world of messages from Jesus and Mary that are constantly reported. The Catholic Church continues to investigate them to inform and safeguard the faithful.

## 19. What is happening in Medjugorje?

The most controversial alleged apparition of the Virgin Mary in the history of the Church comes from the small town of Medjugorje in Bosnia-Herzegovina. Mary—the *Gospa*, as she's affectionately known there—allegedly promised ten secrets to the six seers who were children when they claimed to have begun receiving daily visions in 1981. They have continued to report them on a less frequent basis since 1989, depending on whether they had already received the full set of secrets.

Medjugorje has become a thriving center of pilgrimage, more than thirty million people having visited since the apparitions were reported. Supporters of the apparitions hold up myriad spiritual fruits—physical and spiritual healings, vocations, conversions, and more frequent reception of the sacraments—as proof of authenticity. Pilgrims also claim to experience other miracles, such as solar phenomena, at the apparition site.

In an October 2013 letter from the apostolic nuncio to the United States, writing on behalf of CDF prefect Gerhard Cardinal Müller to the general secretary of the United States Conference of Catholic Bishops, he states: "No cleric or faithful may participate in any meetings, conferences, or public celebrations in which the authenticity of the apparitions is taken for granted."[54] Likewise, the public speaking activities of the seers has been limited until the Vatican renders a further decision.

Paramount in the determination of authenticity is the Virgin's alleged promise of a permanent sign. On March 26, 2010, Pope Benedict XVI assembled a Vatican investigative commission, headed by Cardinal Camillo Ruini and composed of fifteen members of various disciplines. The commission reviewed thousands of messages attributed to the Virgin over thirty years, interviewed all the seers, and on January 18, 2014, gave its report to Pope Francis.

A year and a half later, the pope told reporters, "We've reached the point of making a decision,"[55] but the announcement has been delayed. Speculation on the pope's stance regarding Medjugorje centers on his strong Marian devotion and his caution against basing one's faith solely on predicted visions or anything other than Christ himself. On at least two occasions he has emphasized that the Virgin Mary is not a "postmistress" delivering daily messages.

The establishment and conclusion of the Vatican commission came after much scientific testing throughout the years, the negative judgments by local bishops Pavao Zanic (bishop from 1980 to 1993) and current bishop Ratko Peric, and the Yugoslavian bishops commission rendering the 1991 Zadar declaration of the events not showing proof of supernaturality (though not condemning them):

> The bishops, from the very beginning, have been following the events of Medjugorje through the bishop of the diocese [Mostar], the bishop's commission, and the Commission of the Bishops Conference of Yugoslavia on Medjugorje.
>
> *On the basis of the investigations so far it cannot be affirmed that one is dealing with supernatural apparitions and revelations* [emphasis added].
>
> However, the numerous gatherings of the faithful from different parts of the world who come to Medjugorje, prompted both by motives of belief and various other motives, require the attention and pastoral care in the first place of the diocesan bishop and with him of the other bishops also, so that in Medjugorje and in everything connected

with it a healthy devotion to the Blessed Virgin Mary may be promoted in accordance with the teaching of the Church.

For this purpose the bishops will issue especially suitable liturgical-pastoral directives. Likewise, through their commission they will continue to keep up with and investigate the entire event in Medjugorje.[56]

On February 11, 2017, Pope Francis sent a special envoy, Archbishop Henryk Hoser of Warsaw-Prague, Poland, to assess the pastoral situation without the goal of assessing the reality of the supernatural events.

## 20. How can approved private revelations help me grow closer to God?

For all the dangers that looking for private revelation may involve—ranging from engaging with something that is contrary to the teachings of the Church to simply being distracted from a healthy practice of faith centered on Jesus Christ—these special instances of God's benevolent interference in our world can be a great jumping-off point for strengthening our faith.

For those times when we have spiritual doubts, or simply need that extra push toward God, miraculous events can quench a deep and authentic thirst to know what is good and true. Miracles remind us that God is truly there, looking out as a father for the well-being and protection of his children.

The rich history of the supernatural may attract some to the Church in the first place or may open their hearts to faith in a way they have never before experienced. For young people especially, who find characterizations of the supernatural in popular books, movies, and video games, the realization that the Catholic Church offers real examples of supernatural phenomena may open the door to a more profound experience of God.

We believe in miracles as part of the Christian experience—in at least two miracles, the Incarnation and the Resurrection—and we should keep that openness to continuing divine intervention. Many great saints have experienced private revelation, providing not only examples of holiness that we can try to emulate but acting as bridges between the divine and us.

It is worth noting that the Catholic Church embraces miracles and doesn't consider them vestiges of a superstitious, less-scientific past. It should be reassuring that the Church does not endorse everything that might seem to be miraculous at first blush but instead performs serious investigations when necessary to provide the appropriate pastoral care, protecting us from claims that are unworthy of belief or that could endanger our souls.

There is also comfort in knowing that we are not obligated by our faith to embrace anything related to private revelation, even famous approved examples that feature canonized visionaries and feast days in our Church. It is up to us to decide whether engaging with approved private revelation will benefit our spiritual life.

## About the Author

Michael O'Neill is a miracle researcher and creator of the website MiracleHunter.com, the Web's top resource on Marian apparitions. A graduate of Stanford University and member of the Mariological Society of America, O'Neill has been interviewed about his research in Catholic outlets such as the Catholic Channel and EWTN as well as for secular media, including Fox News, Live Science, and the *Dr. Oz Show*. He is the host of the weekly Relevant Radio program *The Miracle Hunter* and author of *365 Days with Mary* and *Exploring the Miraculous*. He is also the creator of the EWTN docuseries *They Might Be Saints*, about the canonization miracles of the saints, airing in 2017.

# Endnotes

1  Joseph Cardinal Ratzinger, Post-synodal apostolic exhortation *Verbum Domini*, vatican.va/holy_father/benedict_xvi/apost_exhortations/documents/hf_ben-xvi_exh_20100930_verbum-domini_en.html.

2  Ralph M. McInerny, *Miracles: A Catholic View* (Huntington, IN: Our Sunday Visitor, 1986), 121.

3  *Vatican Council II: The Conciliar and Post Conciliar Documents. Denzinger-Schonmetzer*, no. 3034 ; quoted in McInerny, *Miracles*, 121.

4  The IHS Christogram is a monogram or combination of letters that forms an abbreviation for the name of Jesus Christ, traditionally used as a Christian symbol. (*Wikipedia*).

5  "O my Jesus, forgive us our sins, save us from the fires of hell. Lead all souls to heaven, especially those most in need of thy mercy." World Apostolate of Fatima, wafusa.org/the-apostolate/prayers.

6  Tom Doyle with Greg Webster, *Dreams and Visions: Is Jesus Awakening the Muslim World?* (Nashville: Thomas Nelson, 2012), 139.

7  "Mother Teresa of Calcutta," Vatican website, vatican.va/news_services/liturgy/saints/ns_lit_doc_20031019_madre-teresa_en.html, accessed August 3, 2015.

8  "Testimony of the Right Reverend A. Caillot, Bishop of Grenoble, Following the Report Prepared During the Canonical Enquiry into the Case of Mother Eugenia," in *The Father Speaks to His Children* (L'Aquila, Italy: Edizioni Nidi di Preghiera, 1995), 5-10, fatherspeaks.net/pdf/the_father_speaks_english_v-2005-02.pdf.

9  Ibid., 2.

10 "Approved for Faith Expression," The Miracle Hunter, miraclehunter.com/marian_apparitions/approved_apparitions/faith-expression.html, November 2016.

11 EWTN, "Pope Entrusts Rwandan Reconciliation to Our Lady of Kibeho," April 4, 2014, ewtn.com/v/news/getstory.asp?number=129117.

12 "The Virgin Mary Is Not a Postmistress, Who Sends Messages Every Day," Vatican Insider, lastampa.it/2013/11/14/vaticaninsider/eng/the-vatican/the-virgin-mary-is-not-a-postmistress-who-sends-messages-every-day-HqxAjVkrFVzfDHLdkkbLtM/pagina.html, November 11, 2014.

13 Garrigou-Lagrange, *The Three Ages of the Spiritual Life* II, 575–588.

14 St. Teresa of Avila, *Interior Castle*, 6.9.

15 Fr. William G. Most, "Private Revelations and Discernment of Spirits," EWTN, ewtn.com/faith/teachings/maryd8.htm, accessed November 2016.

16 Fr. Benedict J. Groeschel, *A Still, Small Voice: A Practical Guide on Reported Revelations* (San Francisco: Ignatius Press, 1993), 29.

17 "Norms Regarding the Manner of Proceeding in the Discernment of Presumed Apparitions or Revelations," vatican.va/roman_curia/congregations/cfaith/documents/rc_con_cfaith_doc_19780225_norme-apparizioni_en.html, Vatican website, accessed May 24, 2012

18 *Etoile Notre Dame*, October, 2006.

19 General Audience, http://w2.vatican.va/content/benedict-xvi/en/audiences/2010/documents/hf_ben-xvi_aud_20100901.html, September 1, 2010.

20 St. Margaret Mary, Autobiography, in Most, "Private Revelations."

21  Ibid.

22  Maria Faustina Kowalska, *Diary: Divine Mercy in My Soul*, 3rd ed. (Stockbridge, MA: Marian Press, 2005), 365.

23  St. Birgitta (Bridget) of Sweden claimed to have received a great amount of spiritual knowledge mystically infused in an instant and therefore could not necessarily capture it all in writing.

24  Not only must the faithful follow the guidance of the bishop in these matters, but the alleged mystics and their corresponding organizations must be open to the guidance of authority. Sometimes the process is imperfect, considering a local bishop may be personally biased against a certain miraculous claim or may want to limit the distraction that such phenomena can bring. A sensible rule of thumb might be: a superior may or may not be inspired by God in his command, but you are always inspired in obeying.

25  National Conference of Catholic Bishops, *Behold Your Mother: Woman of Faith*, pastoral letter on the Blessed Virgin Mary,  November 21, 1973.

26  October 13, 1996, Radio Renascensa Interview at Fatima, Cardinal Joseph Ratzinger.

27  "Tre Fontane Italy (1947)," The Miracle Hunter, miraclehunter. com/marian_apparitions/approved_apparitions/trefontane, accessed December 2016.

28  René Laurentin and Patrick Sbalchiero, *Dizionario delle apparizioni della vergine Maria* (Rome: Edizione Art, 2010).

29  The Miracle Hunter, miraclehunter.com/marian_apparitions/ approved_apparitions/bishop.html, accessed July 2014.

30  "Claims of Apparitions of Mary Met with Skepticism, Book

Shows," Catholic News Service, December 16, 2010, catholicnews. com/data/stories/cns/1005079.htm, accessed July 2014.

31 Janice T. Connell, "The Spiritual Journey of George Washington," CreateSpace Independent Publishing Platform, September 30, 2013, beliefnet.com/inspiration/angels/2003/02/george-washington-and-the-angel.aspx?p=2.

32 Synod of Bishops, Special Assembly for America, *Encounter with the Living Jesus Christ: The Way to Conversion, Communion, and Solidarity in America*, August 8, 1996, 33, vatican.va/ roman_curia/synod/documents/rc_synod_doc_01081996_usa-lineam_en.html.

33 "Rue du Bac, France (1830)," The Miracle Hunter, miraclehunter. com/marian_apparitions/approved_apparitions/ruedubac.

34 Ibid.

35 Ibid.

36 Joan Carroll Cruz, *The Incorruptibles: A Study of the Incorruption of the Bodies of Various Catholic Saints and Beati* (Rockford, IL: TAN Books, 1977), 34.

37 "4 Literally Awesome Facts About Our Lady of Guadalupe," Mountain Catholic, mtncatholic.com/2014/12/11/4-literally-awesome-facts-about-our-lady-of-guadalupe.

38 Philip Serna Callahan, *The Tilma Under Infra-Red Radiation*, CARA Studies on Popular Devotion, vol. II, Guadalupan Studies 3 (1981).

39 "Report of the Episcopal Commission," The Miracle Hunter, miraclehunter.com/marian_apparitions/statements/lourdes_comm_report.html, accessed December 2016.

40 Theodore Mangiapan, "Les Guérisons de Lourdes: Étude et critique depuis l'origine á nos jours," *Oeuvre de la Grotte* (May 1994).

41 "Lourdes: 69th Official Miracle Announced," Independent Catholic News, indcatholicnews.com/news. php?viewStory=22985.

42 Lucia dos Santos, Fourth Memoir.

43 R. De Marchi, *Témoignages sur les apparitions de Fatima* (France: Missoes Consolata, 1966), 346.

44 "The Revelations of the Two Hearts in Modern Times" (ewtn. com/library/MARY/FIRSTSAT.HTM), accessed December 2016.

45 Pope John Paul II, *Crossing the Threshold of Hope* (New York: Alfred A. Knopf, 1994), 131.

46 "Zeitun, Egypt (1968–71)," MiracleHunter.com, miraclehunter. com/marian_apparitions/approved_apparitions/zeitun/index. html, accessed November 2016.

47 "Zeitun, Egypt (1968–71)," MiracleHunter.com, miraclehunter. com/marian_apparitions/statements/zeitun_02.html, accessed November 2016.

48 "Coptic Approved Apparitions," MiracleHunter.com, miraclehunter.com/marian_apparitions/approved_apparitions/ coptic.html, accessed November 2016.

49 "Approval Sun Carillo Gritti Bispo Prelado Rua," The Miracle Hunter, miraclehunter.com/marian_apparitions/statements/ index.html#itapiranga, accessed November 2016.

50 "Statement from Archbishop Ramon Arguelles," The Miracle Hunter, miraclehunter.com/marian_apparitions/statements/ lipa_statement_03.html.

51 "April 11, 1951: Declaration of Not Supernatural," The Miracle Hunter, miraclehunter.com/marian_apparitions/statements/ lipa_statement_1951.html, accessed December 2016.

52  "September 12, 2015 — Raymond C. Arguelles, Archbishop of Lipa," The Miracle Hunter, miraclehunter.com/marian_apparitions/statements/lipa-arguelles-20150912.html, accessed December 2016.

53  Decree on "Presumed Apparitions of the BVM at the Carmelite Covent in Lipa, Philippines," The Miracle Hunter, miraclehunter.com/marian_apparitions/statements/PROT-N-226-1949.pdf, accessed December 2016.

54  Letter from the Apostolic Nunciature, United States of America, PN 3980, October 23, 2013, ewtn.com/expert/answers/Medjugorje2013.png, accessed January 2017.

55  Carol Glatz, "Vatican Ready to Announce Decision on Medjugorje, Says Pope Francis," Catholic Herald, June 8, 2015, catholicherald.co.uk/news/2015/06/08/vatican-ready-to-announce-decision-on-medjugorje-says-pope-francis, accessed March 2016.

56  miraclehunter.com/marian_apparitions/statements/medjugorje_statement_01.html.